YOUR KNOWLEDGE

Paul Houghton

The training experiences and competence in an IAPT service of recently qualified therapists

GRIN Publishing

Bibliographic information published by the German National Library:

The German National Library lists this publication in the National Bibliography; detailed bibliographic data are available on the Internet at http://dnb.dnb.de .

Imprint:

Copyright © 2007 GRIN Verlag GmbH
Print and binding: Books on Demand GmbH, Norderstedt Germany
ISBN: 978-3-656-89099-7

GRIN - Your knowledge has value

Since its foundation in 1998, GRIN has specialized in publishing academic texts by students, college teachers and other academics as e-book and printed book. The website www.grin.com is an ideal platform for presenting term papers, final papers, scientific essays, dissertations and specialist books.

Visit us on the internet:

http://www.grin.com/

http://www.facebook.com/grincom

http://www.twitter.com/grin_com

How do recently qualified therapists view their training experiences and competence in an IAPT service?

Paul Houghton

Abstract

Following the introduction of the Improving Access to Psychological Therapies Initiative, the author was interested in examining how newly qualified High Intensity Therapists' viewed their training in Cognitive Behavioural Therapy. The author was also interested in exploring their perception of competence to carry out CBT in an IAPT Service following their training. This exploratory study focused on identifying the whole trainee experience and attempted to elicit how they interpreted their personal journey of learning. Interpretative Phenomological Analysis (IPA) was used to analyse data gathered from semi-structured interviews with nine trainee High-Intensity Therapists at the end of a PgDip IAPT CBT Programme. There were three superordinate themes identified – Negative Affect, Loss of Therapist Self, and Loss of Control. There were also several subordinate themes derived from the data. There were several theory/practice gaps identified by the trainees' which they felt needed to be addressed, but there were also elements of their training they considered to be helpful. The range of emotions the trainees' experienced was discussed highlighting mainly negative evaluations of their interpretation of the training on an interpersonal level, but these were influenced by organisational concerns and the clinical placements in which they worked. These issues repeatedly arose for the trainees highlighting the need to address the training or placement/organisational aspects that did not help the trainee and newly qualified therapist working in the IAPT Services. A critical analysis of the results is offered as are limitations of the study together with implications for practice and recommendations for further research.

Introduction

Whilst the High-Intensity Therapist (HIT) training is a new concept, measuring outcomes of therapist competence is not new (Kazantzis, 2003; Tepka et al, 2004; Brosan et al, 2006; Keen and Freeston, 2008; Roth and Pilling, 2008; Davidson and Scott, 2009; Bennett-Levy, et al (2009). Neither is evaluating student experiences of their training programme (Glen and Waddington, 1998; Bennett-Levy and Beedie, 2007; Grant et al, 2008). However, with the introduction of Improving Access to Psychological Therapies (IAPT) there has been a national drive since the publication of the Layard Report in 2006 to implement a structured training programme (Layard, 2006). The reason for this was a lack of qualified therapists working in the NHS and the greater public need for treatment of anxiety and depression, which has been shown to cause significant unemployment and lost revenue (Layard, 2006). At approximately the same time there was a publication after a joint initiative between the

1

National Institute of Mental Health in England (NIMHE) and the Royal College of Psychiatrists who looked at work-force developments and New Ways of Working (NIMHE, 2007). Concerns were raised prior to this regarding psychiatrists who had trained in CBT but were not allowed time to practice in therapy or have appropriate supervision in CBT (Whitfield et al, 2006). Connolly and Brown, (2009) support this argument and highlight that increasing pressures from employers on Consultants would not bring the best desired outcome for improved access to psychological therapies. Hence the drive therefore to train up a workforce in CBT from other disciplines.

This paper is exploring a relatively new area in that the focus is to examine the trainees' experiences of this programme of study, and their perception of competence to work as therapists upon qualification in an IAPT Service. Owing to this being a new area under examination, the literature is quite sparse concerning the IAPT Training Programme and its evaluation. Milne (1985) examined 17 empirical studies concerning the training of psychiatric and mental handicap nurses in behavioural therapy. It was highlighted how training needed to be systematically investigated to address the gap between specific training interventions and institutional constraints. Kazantzis, (2003) examined the empirical evidence for CB Therapists' competence and found the psychometric measures to be mixed and there were inadequate demonstrations of inter-rater reliability including those of experts in the field. Brosan et al, (2006) found that if the trainee appraised supervision in CBT as a negative process then this would have a direct effect on eroding their skills. Keen and Freeston, (2008) argued for more supervision of cases of the trainees' and highlighted problems in reliability and validity in assessment procedures. Owing to this issue the Competency Map developed by Roth and Pilling (2008) was implemented into the IAPT Training protocol as a means to better identifying trainee development through the course. Davidson and Scott, (2009) identified that therapists differ in the effectiveness in how they deliver psychological therapies. They went on to examine if there was any variance in the trainees' professional background as to how they delivered therapy. Bennett-Levy et al, (2009) found that whilst there was evidence to suggest that CBT training and supervision could enhance therapist skills, the specific training techniques for the development of CBT was lacking.

With regards to experiences of their training both Glen and Waddington, (1998) and Robinson et al, (2012) examined the transition of the nurse into specialist roles including that of IAPT High Intensity Therapist. Grant et al, (2008) explored the transfer of the trainee from classroom to clinical setting and how for this transition to take place effectively there would need to be more collaborative working between the educational establishments and health organisations.

Measuring competence in CBT is not on the face of it an easy task and there have been calls for further developments in this area (Keen and Freeston, 2008; Shafran, et al, 2009). Keen and Freeston (2008) argue procedures employed by Universities to measure trainee competence in CBT have relatively low reliability which in turn imposes a low upper limit on validity. It is argued that there needs to be more close supervision of cases to address this issue, but it is also highlighted how resources do not allow for this to take place. To add

2

weight to this argument, Shafran et al (2009) also state how therapy is not easy to evaluate in terms of trainee competence. It is argued that more research needs to take place with regards to both competence and adherence as treatment quality can be obtained by using both of these measures. It is put that adherence to CBT principles demonstrate that the trainee is doing what they should be doing, whilst competence refers to the quality of the therapy which is being delivered (Shafran et al, 2009). Shafran et al (2009) summarise the skill level needed by trainees to obtain effective treatment outcomes should be identified.

In going some way to address this, Roth and Pilling developed a Competency Map so both trainee and supervisor could assess the student's skill-level in CBT. There are five competency domains: Basic CBT competencies, specific CBT techniques, problem-specific competencies, and meta-competencies (Roth and Pilling, 2008). However, a problem here is that the trainee may over-rate their abilities and the supervisor may be rating the trainees' abilities after only seeing several snap-shots of their practice. Indeed, Zivor et al (2013) found a gap between self-appraisal and actual performance when examining clinicians' perception of competence both before and after a skills work-shop in CBT formulation. Likewise, assessing the trainee using the Cognitive Therapy Rating Scale Revised (CTS-R) can be seen as a method that is not without question. However, assessors meet every six months at the University in which the participants studied in an attempt to calibrate marking.

Bennett-Levy and Beedie (2007) examined students' perception of competence during cognitive therapy training and found that the trainees' self-perception of competence changed over time. It was highlighted how this varied considerably between different skills and between individuals. It is highlighted that whilst there is little evidence to ascertain if therapist competence is associated with better treatment outcomes, it is argued high or low confidence of the therapist is related to actual therapeutic performance (Bennette-Levy and Beedie, 2009). This highlights once again the importance of assessing the trainees' appraisal of their actual competence, but, also to assess their perception regarding their confidence.

Bennett-Levy and Beedie (2009 p. 26) further put

'*If researchers can understand the process of training better, then it may be possible to alleviate some of the stress sand doubts about competence that may impact on therapist performance and patient outcomes, and may sometimes affect trainees' emotional wellbeing*'.

Clinical supervision has been highlighted by the participants as a very helpful component of their training and development as therapists. However, it would be important to examine which aspects of supervision were the most helpful so these could be replicated, but that is out of the scope of this paper. In saying that, Gonsalve and Freestone (2007) highlight at times there may be a 'leniency bias' in supervision in which the supervisor goes easy on the trainee when evaluating their performance. In contrast to this, as highlighted by Brosan et al (2006), if the trainee were to find supervision to be a negative process and felt criticised by their supervisor then this too could have a negative impact on their development. So the key word here is 'balance' – supervision should be delivered so that it stretches and supports the trainee, in line with The Zone of Proximal Development (Doolittle, 1997), but it should not be a process where constructive questioning is absent.

If the trainee has a positive view regarding their supervision they are more likely to evaluate their skills and self-efficacy more favourably (Borders, 1990; Cashwell and Dooley, 2001). However, their perception of skill is not an indicator of their competence so again this is something that needs to be explored with the trainee.

The IAPT training programme was not only concerned with recruiting mental health nurses. Many of the now qualified therapists are from various backgrounds from Psychologists, Social Workers, Occupational Therapists and those who worked prior as Psychological Well-being Practitioners. Davidson and Scott (2009) found that despite professional background or qualification there were no relationships in therapist competence. In the author's experience however, when supervising trainees and newly qualified therapists, a difference has been noticed between how therapists from different backgrounds practice CBT more globally. For example, mental health nurses have been trained in psychiatry and the medical model and therefore had knowledge of psychotropic medication and were more proactive in liaising with GPs and psychiatrists regarding this.

Method

Nine newly qualified High-Intensity Therapists took part in a semi-structured interview lasting one hour. All therapists were working in Primary Care and had recently completed their training. The therapists were purposefully selected from local IAPT Primary Care Mental Health Teams. They were all contacted by the author after a request was sent to their line manger as advised by the NHS Trust Research and Development advisor. When permission was granted an email was sent to the HITs outlining the study with an 'Opt-In Pack' attached including a consent form for them to sign and send back to the author for those wishing to take part in the study (Appendix).

Once recruitment was completed the trainees were interviewed and these were audio recorded and transcribed and data was analysed using Interpretative Phenomological Analysis to extract themes of their experiences. The interview questions were piloted with an earlier cohort of IAPT trainees to confirm the questions were appropriate to answer the research question. Some questions were discarded before the interviews and some were not used at interview owing to a cross-over of answers which resulted in the latter question being answered by the trainee with the former one. Prompts were used such as, 'can you elaborate on that', or, 'Can I check what you mean here' to gain clarity of meaning and understanding. Smith and Osborn (2003) support the use of prompts and advise on the testing out of interview questions to get feedback and to check the difficulty of question and tone. Smith and Osborn (2003) also state that not all questions need to be asked by the interviewer, nor asked in the same way. It is basically up to the interviewer's intuition if a certain question has already been answered or if a particular question fits the schedule of what the participant is saying.

Design

This was an exploratory study carrying out semi-structured interviews with nine newly qualified High-Intensity Therapists lasting one hour. The interviews were audio-recorded and transcribed. Interpretative Phenomological Analysis (IPA) (Smith et al, 2009) was used as a method to both capture and analyse data and to extract themes and meanings pertaining to the trainees' experiences of the training programme they under-took. The questions are aimed at eliciting both helpful and not so helpful elements of their training, and their perceptions of how competent they felt as therapists.

Participants

The participants were purposefully selected from local NHS IAPT Service teams who were nearing the end of a PgDIP CBT training programme (IAPT Curriculum). The ratio of female to male participants was 7:2 with a mean age of 31.5 years. 13 trainees were approached and nine agreed to take part with a response rate of 69.23%.

The nine participants identified numerically to protect confidentiality:

Participant	Age	Designation
P1	31	CBT Trainee NHS
P2	34	CBT Trainee NHS
P3	31	CBT Trainee NHS
P4	27	CBT Trainee NHS
P5	28	CBT Trainee NHS
P6	27	CBT Trainee NHS
P7	28	CBT Trainee NHS
P8	36	CBT Trainee NHS
P9	27	CBT Trainee NHS

Fig 1

Ethical Considerations

All participants were given a leaflet explaining what the study was concerned with and given a consent form to sign. Ethical approval was granted from the author's NHS Trust to go ahead with the study. Participants were encouraged to ask further questions about the study and interview process. They were informed that they could drop out of the study at any time and that confidentiality would be maintained. Field and Hole (2003) state it is fundamental that participants are fully informed about what the study involves, their right to confidentiality and how they should be protected from physical or psychological harm. The author gave adequate information to the participants which was overseen by the Trust's Research and Development representative.

Data Analysis

This analysis was conducted with reference to Smith, Flowers and Larkin (2009) Interpretative Phenomological Analysis (IPA). Data was gathered from the semi-structured interviews. The transcripts were read and re-read to familiarise the researcher with the data. Smith et al, (2009) state it is important to become as intimate as possible with the account as each reading could result in new insights. Anything the participants said which was of interest or felt to be significant was highlighted with a highlighter pen to identify possible subordinate themes. Once this was completed, the text was re-read and potential superordinate themes were highlighted in a different colour. The emergent themes were then listed on a separate pieces of paper to identify any connections between them. Smith et al (2009) state when carrying out this clustering procedure, themes and associate or master themes can be identified.

When looking for emergent themes Smith et al (2009) state the task of managing the data changes as the analyst reduces the volume of detail slowly moving away from the transcripts to the initial notes. As interrelationships, connections and patterns emerged, the author was able to put aside the transcripts and focus mainly on the initial notes making further notes and putting aside any information that did not seem to 'fit' with the rest of the data. It was a long and laborious process but the author was trying to elicit meaning of the trainees' experience and was attempting to understand what they were saying but also feeling as well, i.e. how were they interpreting their experience. Smith et al (2009 P.92) further put that themes are usually expressed as phrases which 'speak the psychological essence of the piece', and that capturing what is crucial within this should be the focus of analysis, but one should also allow oneself to be influenced by the whole text as well. This is a hermeneutic cycle in that the crucial parts captured from the text are influenced by the whole text with regards to interpretation and the whole text is interpreted by the part (Smith et al, 2009). Smith and Osborn (2003) state the researcher needs to be disciplined to discern repeated patterns, but also acknowledge any new material which arises when reading through the scripts. So whilst there was a systematic process being carried out, none of the data was discounted, only put aside once it was felt all crucial data had been gathered.

The author attempted to apply a 'clear and enquiring mind' when looking at the data over a period of time. The whole process took some time and the data was revisited on several occasions. For example, the author became very familiar with the data by looking at it during the week, or 'in work mode', and also looking at it at other times, 'off time'. It is felt that this process allowed a more in-depth understanding of the trainees' world and experiences. The author felt a connection with the trainees' and attempted to 'feel and think as they did'. Of course the author has also been through several areas of training so could apply some personal and retrospective empathy towards the trainees' meanings.

It was initially a 'messy process' involving lots of paper and floor-space, but over time this was funnelled down to just two pieces of paper with the decided and chosen emergent themes. The author also used Atlas TI as a means to identifying the most used words to help with the sorting and partitioning of data.

IPA takes a hermeneutic stance which involves inquiry and trying to understand the meaning of an experience by a person or group (Larkin et al, 2006). In doing this, it is hoped that a better understanding could be observed of the participant's personal world or as Conrad (1987) puts it, an 'insider' perspective. Basically, the trainees were encouraged to make sense of their experiences and the author was attempting to make sense of the trainees' making sense of their experience by looking for a chain of connection between what they said, what they thought and what motional state they experienced (Smith and Osborne, 2003). This process is very similar to the CBT approach so it is felt both the author and trainee were comfortable with this line of enquiry. Smith et al (2009) state there is no definitive way to carry out IPA so the author did use both systematic and interpersonal processes to try and get a better understanding of what the trainees' meant when answering questions. With regards to sample size Smith and Osborn (2003) state IPA usually involves small sizes and in doing so one is sacrificing breadth for depth with regards to data gathered and analysed.

Several subordinate themes were identified from the data gathered. Trainees experienced several emotional responses during the semi-structured interviews including: anxiety, anger, frustration, worry, confusion, sadness, a sense of loss, despair, feeling both under and over-whelmed, a sense of dread, feeling unsatisfied, hurt and betrayed. There were three superordinate, or master themes identified from the data: **Negative Affect** which was an interpersonal process the trainees' experienced, **Loss of Therapist Self**, considered to be a 'felt sense' and both an interpersonal and cognitive process influenced by the external factors of teaching and work placement, and **Loss of Control** again considered to be a 'felt sense' with both interpersonal and cognitive processes being mainly influenced by their experiences in their clinical placements, i.e. Working in an IAPT Service.

The author tried to separate the emotions (Negative Affect) from the other two superordinate themes because whilst they do over-lap, emotions can 'get in the way' as it were if 'allowed' to take over the analysis. It was considered necessary to partition the Loss of Therapist Self and Loss of Control as separate entities as these were more of a 'felt sense' (intuition) experienced by the trainees incorporating cognitions associated with specific academic and work components of the analysis.

Intuition is not easy to define but it has been examined with regards to nursing practice (Benner 1987; McCutcheon and Pincombe, 2001; Truman, 2003). McCutcheon and Pincombe state Intuition is an understanding of the concept based on feelings, knowledge and experience. Truman (2003) argues although intuition cannot be scientifically measured, it is still invaluable tool for professionals to use. The author felt intuition was appropriate as a term as it accessed a deeper level of meanings the trainees' gave regarding their experiences. It was also felt that as therapists they should have a developing 'intuiting self' and it was hoped that this may be used to good effect for the study.

Superordinate Theme	Subordinate Theme
1) **Negative Affect (NA)** – Interpersonal Process	**Emotion and Meaning:** Anxiety, anger, frustration, worry, confusion, sadness, loss, despair, underwhelmed, overwhelmed, dread, unsatisfied, uncertainty, hurt, betrayed.
2) **Loss of Therapist Self (LOTS)** – Interpersonal Process/External Factor	**Teaching, Gaps In Knowledge/Experience:** To accomplish a competent therapist self, trainees appraised this as needing: More training on specific disorders, More live demonstrations of therapy, having access to Clients with specific disorders to consolidate learning, More teaching on working with co-morbidity and complex cases. More supervision. Longer course duration.
3) **Loss of Control – (LOC)** Interpersonal Process/External Factor	**Organisational and Service Demand:** Trainees felt controlled in their practice and hindered in learning through: Working within a 12-session format, Expectation to see Clients so early in the course, Amount of clinical hours expected of trainees', Expected to work with complex cases outside of IAPT remit – anxiety and depression in Step Three. Having access to Clients with specific disorders to coincide with training.

Fig 2

Emotions the trainees felt during the course became apparent during the interviews. Most of the emotions expressed were mainly negative such as anxiety, anger, frustration, and worry. However, there were some positive emotions experienced by the trainees. The trainees reported anxieties about their ability to practice in the IAPT Services and most felt the training did not prepare them for this. There was also a common theme of anxiety and frustration regarding their clinical placements and what was expected of them by the organisation. However, all of the above could be considered as normal cognitive and emotional processing during training in a new area for trainees. The IAPT Programme is an intense and very prescriptive area of teaching and training so one would assume affect in trainees would be fairly strong.

What follows will be a systematic analysis of the interview questions and pertinent segments of the answers the trainees gave in the semi-structured interviews, with a summary highlighting valid points and themes with regards to their perception of experience.

Interview Question:

How competent do you feel with regards to your training to carry out CBT? – **NA, LOTS and LOC.**

P1. 'I feel like a novice, but I also feel pressure to be competent'. 'Hitting service targets make it hard to develop practice'.

P2. 'I feel sort of competent but not satisfied with my practice'. 'There was lots of pressure at work'.

P3. 'At first I felt enthusiastic then unsure'. 'We had to have 12 contacts a week straight away – 4 per day'.

P4. 'I still feel like a novice'. 'There are lots of new ways of working to learn'. 'I need more time to consolidate'.

P5. 'I don't feel competent'. 'I know the theory but need time to consolidate practice'.

P6. 'I haven't had the experience of working with all of the disorders and didn't expect to be working with OCD and PTSD so early'.

P7. 'Generally okay'. 'We worked with most disorders in training'. 'I feel fairly competent'.

P8. 'I feel I know all of the models'. 'I feel pretty competent'. 'I feel I have the skills to treat the vast majority of Clients, but I need a couple of years to develop'.

P9. 'I feel 50% competent'. 'I feel the Clients we see are more complex than what we were trained for'. 'There is no such thing as the IAPT Client, people don't fit boxes'. 'If IAPT was a person I would torture them'.

Most of the trainees' felt they were not competent when asked this direct question regarding their clinical ability. Two of the trainees however considered themselves to be competent practitioners. Feelings of pressure and anxiety together with anger are apparent and there does seem to be elements of frustration experienced by the trainee highlighting mainly NA. There is also realisation from some of the trainees that they need to take some responsibility for their own continued learning in the areas they feel were lacking. There are organisational issues that have been highlighted with regards to service targets and the pressure the trainee

9

feels working in the IAPT Services which shows a LOC. Having access to Clients with specific disorders concurrent with the appropriate teaching modules was also an issue causing the trainee some concern. They all seem to accept that they have a good theoretical knowledge, but the practical components appear to be lacking which causes in turn a LOTS.

The second question was used to elicit more direct information associated with the trainee's perception of their training to work in the IAPT Services:

Interview Question:

Was the training sufficient for you to be able to work effectively in primary care? – **LOTS LOC AND NA.**

P1. 'No, but it wasn't the lecturer's fault'. 'The group came from diverse mental health backgrounds and some had no experience of working in Primary Care'.

P2. 'A bit'. 'It all made sense at Uni, but Clients don't fit into models'.

P3. 'Yes'. 'We covered all aspects of IAPT'. 'I rate the course but the IAPT Programme doesn't fit the reality of Primary Care'. 'Most of the Clients are more complex'.

P4. 'No.' 'The course was based around Clients with clear presentations and no complexities'. 'It does not reflect the real world'.

P5. 'Training needs to be geared towards working within 12 sessions'. 'I am not very good at identifying diagnoses'.

P6. 'During training no, now yes'.

P7. 'Yes'.

P8. 'Yes, to a degree'. 'However, I feel it is necessary to have a background in mental health before training'.

P9. 'There was a massive gap in theory and practice and the service needs seem to depersonalise the Client'.

It is clearly evident from these questions that the majority of trainees' considered a vast difference in the theory and practice of CBT when working within the demands of the IAPT Services. It seems that whilst there was some good teaching taking place at university, the reality of what was expected of the trainee's by their organisation did not quite fit with what they had been taught (LOC and LOTS). Anxieties the trainee's experienced appeared to be based in some confusion between their own view of how they should practice and what they expected from the university and the clinical placements (NA, LOTS, LOC). There are some discrepancies evident between classroom CBT and Primary Care practice. The Client not

10

quite 'fitting' the taught theory seems to be a theme here and the reference made regarding depersonalising the Client indicates one of the trainees was feeling some elements of anger, and may feel the Clients were being short-changed with regards to the therapy they received. This could maybe termed a 'Loss of Client – Therapist Self). The prescriptive nature of teaching is highlighted which the trainees did not feel fully reflected the Clients they worked with in the IAPT Services which again caused some negative affect for the trainee.

A further question was used to elicit any precise aspects the trainee's considered to be valuable with regards to their training:

Interview question:

What aspects of your training do you feel were the most effective? – **LOTS.**

P1. 'Watching live sessions of CBT with an OCD Client'. 'Videos of real therapy'.

P2. 'Good teachers gave us hope'. 'We had good trainers'. 'Being shown all of the CBT models'.

P3. 'Skills practice, role-plays, supervision and OSCEs'. 'I got a lot from these, but would have been useful to look at working with more complex Clients'.

P4. 'Being introduced to looking at new ways of working'. 'It was very different form the PWP role and supervision was effective'.

P5. 'Lectures on anxiety disorders and watching live CBT'. 'It would have been useful to have seen live CBT for each disorder and a demonstration of how to work with complex Clients'. 'The Mater Classes were very helpful'.

P6. 'Introduction to the theory and ideas about the development of disorders and their symptoms'.

P7. 'What a safety behaviour is and their subtleties'. 'Lectures on Exposure work and Behavioural Experiments geared towards testing out the Client's beliefs'. 'Role-play and the Trauma Module'.
P8. 'Video sessions and supervision'. 'Using the CTS-R, OSCEs and role-plays'.

P9. 'Presenting theoretical ideas and reflecting on them'. 'Interactive lectures and debate'. 'Supervision and the videoing of sessions'.

It appears from these answers that the trainee's valued highly their experience of the different formats of teaching demonstrating positive affect. It is evident that watching live sessions of CBT was useful as were the active ingredients of *doing* CBT. It is somewhat surprising however that the trainee's seemed to enjoy and benefit from role-play and OSCEs as usually students tend to be anxious about exposing themselves in this way. In the author's opinion it is assumed that this modality of teaching and assessment was effective and delivered well owing to the trainee's responses. It highlights that the trainees' benefit from being shown how to do CBT. It also shows that the trainees' seem to learn more from the active components of lectures. It could be argued that this question elicited both positive affect and a 'Confirmation of Therapist Self' which is diluted somewhat when they enter the IAPT Services.

Although the trainees' highlighted some gaps between theory and practice in the earlier questions, the author asked them this direct question in an attempt to further clarify and elicit any specific areas regarding this:

Interview question:

Where there any gaps between theory and practice? **LOTS, LOC and NA.**

P1. 'Yes, they teach stuff they don't believe in'. 'The training is too prescriptive and needs to be more transdiagnostic'. ' There is a big difference between Uni and work supervision'. 'I feel I have to be more cautious at work'. 'All Clients are idiosyncratic and not all theories of CBT fit the Client'.

P2. 'Yes'. 'The reality of practice to the theory of CBT'. 'There are no straight forward cases in the real world'.

P3. 'Yes'. 'IAPT parameters were underwhelming; They don't fit the real world'. 'You are expected to work with Clients you are not trained to work with such as eating disorders'.

P4. 'People don't fit into models and this is not realistic on the shop floor'. 'We need to consider comorbidity and I felt the transdiagnostic approach fitted pretty well by the end of the course'.

P5. 'Loads'. 'Clients don't fit the theory'. 'Only one model per disorder was taught'. 'Models are for the therapist'.

P6. 'Some Clients don't fit the theory of CBT'.

P7. 'Yes, many'.

P8. 'Clients don't fit the theory of the work we do in the real world of Primary Care'.

P9. 'We need more training in complex cases'. 'Who do we refer to when the CCTT won't accept them'?

All trainees reported a large division between the academic and organisational establishments (LOTS and LOC). It is not surprising therefore they experienced quite high levels of emotion owing to this confusion (NA). It appears there is clear evidence to highlight to trainees how to work with complex cases using a more transdiagnostic approach. Of course this would be the ideal, but we need to consider learning and ability to practice and consolidate learning with one model/disorder at a time as the trainees' may well become overwhelmed if given too much information. This could also result in LOTS. It seems also evident that the organisation has a responsibility in identifying suitable Clients for the trainee to work with (LOC). They seem to all experience Clients with comorbid and complex issues which cause them anxiety and frustration (NA). It also appears that there is no clear care pathway from Step Three to Step Four services thereby making the trainee feel overwhelmed and unsupported by the organisation (LOTS, LOC, NA).

The next question was used to elicit the trainees' views of what changes they would like to see with regards to their CBT curriculum:

Interview question:

What would you change about the curriculum? – **LOTS and LOC.**

P1. 'I feel we should have started seeing Clients later on in training; I felt we started therapy too soon'. 'It would have been better if we could have seen two Clients per day instead of four'. 'I didn't feel I had enough time to consolidate my learning; Service needs got in the way'. 'We were not seen as people and I felt we had no identity'. 'I think an 18-month course with smaller caseloads would have been better'.

P2. 'Not sure'. 'Maybe an 18-month course instead of 12'. 'Maybe have Master Classes earlier in the year'.

P3. 'More training on the realities of working in Primary Care'. 'There was an idealistic view from Uni'. 'The course was crammed and a two-year course would have been better with more supervision'.

P4. 'An 18-month course with more supervision'. 'I felt there was only a whistle-stop tour of the theory of CBT'. 'We had too many contacts to see in a week and we needed more consolidation time'.

P5. 'More teaching on anxiety disorders and more live CBT with demonstrations for each disorder'. 'A longer course of maybe 18-months with more Third Wave stuff'.

P6. 'More practice on the skills of CBT and to see it in practice; More live therapy'. 'A longer course and not to have to see so many Clients so soon after starting the course'.

P7. 'More live CBT by the experts'. 'See them working with complex Clients and making mistakes'.

P8. 'Longer course of 18-months with additional supervision and more skills demonstrations'. 'Seeing qualified CBT Therapists at work and also getting it wrong'.

P9. 'More support for students who are doing self-exposure'. 'We are human beings too'. 'More on how to deal with Clients who project onto the trainees'.

It appears that all trainees' wanted the course to be delivered over a longer period of time with at least an extra six months teaching. They also wanted more clinical supervision and to see CBT demonstrated by experienced clinicians including not always getting it 'right'. It seems the students are looking for some honesty with regards to the discrepancies between teaching and shop floor work (LOC). It seems as if they are losing some belief in the job before they even commence it as qualified therapists (LOTS). They do not seem to feel ready to practice after the year-long course. Most feel there was so much to learn in a short time that is was impossible to offer the Client an appropriate level of skilled therapy (LOTS. One trainee felt the service needs took priority and in some way they appraised this as a loss of identity. It looks as if both confidence and appraisal of competence have been affected by the trainees experiences of their training and clinical practice. Maybe the *process* of *becoming* a therapist should also be included in the curriculum to help normalise and reduce these anxieties in the trainees' and help t promote a stronger sense of therapist self. One reference is made to trainees' not being 'seen' as human beings which clearly demonstrates a further loss of self apart from the LOTS.

The next question was a direct enquiry to extract how the trainee appraised competence and how they could identify specifically with this:

Interview question:

How do you know when you are competent in your role? – **LOTS, NA and LOC.**

P1. 'When I am not taking 20-sessions with a Client'. 'When there is no drift and I am asking the right questions'.
P2. 'When I can develop good treatment plans and can identify the main issue as opposed to working with several diagnoses'. 'Client feedback, MDS Scores and my own confidence'.

P3. 'Good sessions'. 'Not sure if we are ever completely competent'. 'MDS Scores, Client feedback, completed homework, change noted and motivated Client'.

P4. 'When I can reflect more and adapt in session'. 'Read less before a session and see a shift in the Client'.

P5. 'When I feel I have a good understanding of the Client and when they come back'.

P6. 'I feel less anxious'. 'When I have several ideas about how to progress in therapy'.

P7. 'I can identify approaches to treatment more quickly'. 'I can use prior knowledge and reflect'.

P8. 'Feedback from Client and working within 12-sessions'.

P9. 'I go off a feeling if a session goes well'. 'I have less therapeutic drift'.

It appears the trainees' are looking at competence here with regards to working in a time-limited and structured fashion in therapy. References are made to working within 12-sessions and to having less drift and using less preparation time before a session. Some appraise competence when the Client returns for another session whilst others use their own senses or internal processes to gauge competence. Some report to experiencing less anxiety when working with Clients (NA) and another appraises being competent when they have a better understanding of the Client. So both internal and external factors play a part it would seem with regards to how the trainee evaluates their personal competence as therapists. Most responses seem to indicate a LOTS in that the trainees' report to lacking something as therapists owing to needing further input from the university and the service demands of time-limited working.

The next question explored the trainees' feelings towards not feeling competent in their role as therapists:

Are there times when you feel you are not competent? – **NA, LOTS and LOC.**

P1. 'If I've not worked with a disorder before'. 'When I don't know enough'.

P2. 'Yes with certain Clients'. 'I feel less confident with some and find it hard to stop them and keep them on track'.
P3. 'When I have planned the session but the Client goes off focus'.

P4. 'Yes, when I am not assertive with Clients who don't engage. I.e. not do their homework'. 'I don't feel confident working with GAD'.

P5. 'If the person isn't getting better, no shift in scores'.

P6. 'Yes, most of the time'. 'If they don't drop out of therapy'.

P7. 'Yes at times, it varies day to day'. 'When the Client is not making progress or doesn't do homework'.

P8. 'Yes, most of the time'. 'Since going full-time, you get what you get of the waiting list and they are all complex'.

P9. 'Very rarely'. 'Maybe when I am working with a new problem, i.e. a complex Client with a long history'.

Most of the trainees' appear to experience differing levels of anxiety pertaining to their competence (NA). This seems to follow similar issues with regards to Client engagement in therapy and the structure of CBT. Keeping the Client focused seems to be a common problem with newly qualified therapists as does their anxieties when working with a 'new' disorder (NA). Again the perceived complexities of Client's issues seem to be the cause of concern for trainees' working in the IAPT Services (LOTS and LOC). Also one of the trainee's measures not being competent if the Client drops out of therapy or 'doesn't come back' highlighting some personalisation with regards to the ability to practice with such Clients (LOTS). There certainly seems to be a gap here with regards to the structured and 'clean' therapy which is taught, and that of the work in Primary Care in which there is a moderate DNA rate in most services (LOTS and LOC). It may be useful to highlight this within training curriculum to assist in relieving some of the anxieties experienced by trainees in this area. The 'targets' or Service needs seem to be a precursor for the trainees' perception of competence as they seem to get anxious if a Clients MDS Scores do not decrease (NA, LOTS, LOC). In light of this, the author feels some reformulation of cases may be helpful in the training in CBT to sharpen the trainees' skills in this area and reduce anxieties. Also, it may be useful to normalise this highlighting that probably 50% of Clients will make improvement and 50% probably will not show improvement in symptoms, certainly in light of Client complexities and discrepancy between Steps Two and Three as highlighted.

The next question investigated the trainees' views regarding which Clients they found difficult to work with:

Interview question:

Are there any particular Clients you struggle to work with? – **NA, LOTS and LOC.**

P1. 'GAD, lots of comorbidity, personality issues or if CBT is not suitable'

P2. 'Reluctant to engage or if the Client delves in to the past too much'

P3. 'Learned helplessness or secondary gains'.

P4. 'Past Counselling Clients who go off track'. 'PTSD Clients and 'yes but' Clients'.

P5. 'Clients lacking self-efficacy'. 'Clients who don't take responsibility'.

P6. 'PTSD – No experience'.

P7. 'PTSD, Phobias, OCD'.

P8. 'PDs, history of drug abuse. I find it hard to relate to them interpersonally'. 'We were not given training for this'.

P9. 'Step Four Clients on methadone and GAD'.

Interesting to note here is how the trainees' perceived this question. It appears that they see the Client as a 'disorder' or set of diagnoses' as opposed to a unique individual with idiosyncratic presentations. It could be argued that the process of training promotes a sense of 'diagnosis' which in turn may depersonalise the Client and cause a loss for them. Another Interesting observation is how one of the trainees complained of the organisation being to blame for this in an earlier question. Clients appear to be labelled as 'fitting' certain treatment protocols or another service. The author feels the answers to this particular issue warrants further training in working with complex cases for trainees and the skills needed for doing so. There are elements in the answers above whereby it appears the Client is being questioned for the difficulties experienced by the trainee therapist (LOTS). It would be interesting to see how many trainees carry on with therapy despite their thoughts and feelings being somewhat unhelpful, how many reformulate when they face these difficulties, how many cases such as these are brought to supervision. It would also be interesting to explore if the trainee is 'brave' enough to tackle these issues with the Client, themselves and the organisation i.e. when to end therapy, refer to another modality of treatment or service and when to discharge (LOC). Again, in the author's opinion including a session on such issues as 'endings' may be useful in reducing both anxiety (NA) and labelling issues.

The next question did in fact ask about which disorders that trainees' preferred to work with:

Interview question:

Are there any problems you prefer to work with? – **NA and LOTS.**

P1. 'OCD, Social Phobia, GAD and Depression'.

P2. 'OCD, Social Phobia and PTSD'.

P3. 'PTSD, Panic and Health Anxiety'.

P4. 'OCD, GAD, Trauma and Panic'.

P5. 'Depression and Panic'.

P6. 'PTSD, Phobias and OCD'.

P7. 'GAD and Social Phobia'.

P8. 'Depression'.

P9. 'OCD and Panic'.

Disorder/Number	Ranking
OCD – 5	1
PTSD – 4 Panic – 4	2
Social Phobia – 3 GAD – 3 Depression – 3	3
Health Anxiety – 1 Phobias – 1	4

Fig. 3

It is evident here that trainees' much prefer to work with anxiety disorders instead of working with Clients with depression. The majority would prefer to work with Clients diagnosed with OCD. The author is not surprised at this owing to experiences whilst supervising 7 trainees on an earlier IAPT Course. It was evident then that trainees brought a lot of Clients with OCD to supervision for discussion. They tended to get quite anxious the further in therapy they progressed with these particular Clients. They tended to struggle, but their perception was it was a disorder which best 'fitted' the CBT approach. Only later on as practicing clinicians have they found OCD to be a particular difficult disorder to treat and many changed their views regarding preferences on which disorders they chose to work with. It could be argued that this is a normal progression from trainee to more experienced therapist and what seems to be evident with the trainees under study is mirrored by previous trainees and in the author's experience. They eventually develop an identity as a therapist self in the author's opinion.

Another interesting point to note is how health anxiety appeared to be quite low in the 'preferential ranking' when similar therapeutic skills are used as with those Clients suffering from OCD. It would be interesting to determine if the tutors also swayed to working with anxiety disorders, and if this had an influence of preference of which Clients to work with for the trainees. This could obviously put a bias in the newly qualified therapists appraisal of their abilities certainly in the early stages of practice, which the author feels in time does either strengthen or reside. Another point to note would be if the tutors came from more of a behavioural background as opposed to a cognitive stance in therapy. It could be argued that this too could bias how the trainee initially practiced CBT and whether this in turn could influence the preferences discussed with individual trainees. It could also be argued that the trainee will feel less anxiety when taking a referral for a preferred disorder as opposed to a 'new' problem they are less familiar with or, have had a positive experience when working with a previous Client with the same diagnosis, i.e. the Client made improvement, the MDS Scores decrease, they felt as if work was carried out in a structured way, and the trainee completed therapy within the 12-session remit. So there could be LOTS if the trainee is influenced by teaching to work with a particular style if that particular way of working does not fit their personal make-up, i.e. working with more of behavioural style when they feel more confident in cognitive approaches. This can cause NA until the trainee develops and 'takes themselves to CBT' as opposed to doing CBT by the book or how they were shown to do it.

A further question was a direct question to explore which skills the trainee considered to be their most effective in CBT:

Interview question:

What would you say your best skills were in CBT? – **LOTS.**

P1. 'Engagement with the Client, showing empathy, being genuine and using the Core Conditions'.

P2. 'Relationship building, formulation to models. Collaboration, homework-setting, agenda-setting and feedback'.

P3. 'Relationship building and assisting the Client to be able to open up'. Behavioural experiments, preparing for sessions and structure of sessions'.

P4. 'Therapeutic alliance, trusting relationship'.

P5. 'Formulating cases'. 'Systematic approach to treatment'. 'Metaphors, analogies and using the Socratic Method'.

P6. 'Agenda-setting, eliciting key cognitions, emotions and feelings'. 'Therapeutic alliance'.

P7. 'Use of humour and belief in CBT'. 'I sell CBT well'.

P8. 'Interpersonal style and behavioural work'.

P9. 'Relationship building and working with resistive Clients'. 'I use clear language, not jargon'.
It is clear here that all trainees have highlighted the importance of the therapeutic relationship as high on the 'agenda' of necessary skills to be an effective therapist. Answers appear to be referenced to the CTS-R when the trainee considers what their 'best skills' are when working

with Clients. It could be argued that these interpersonal qualities could not be taught and are therefore the make-up of individual trainees' personality and ability to engage with Clients, so maybe the superordinate theme does not fit here too well. It is also interesting to see how the trainees could readily reel off the skills (and qualities not asked for) they thought they used effectively and also conversely in earlier questions they seemed to be unsure about their abilities to practice competently (LOTS). The author argues that the trainee is maybe blinded on occasions regarding their competence as is evident in these answers, i.e. the trainees all seem to have a good understanding of the skills they have, but in some cases 'forget' they have them. It is as though there is a 'practice amnesia' evident which may in turn heighten negative affect and belief in themselves as competent therapists.

The next question was a very specific CBT question asking the trainee to 'measure' the skills they thought to be effective:

Interview question:

How do you measure this? – **LOTS.**

P1. 'By my feelings and instinct'. 'How the Client presents and what they say'.

P2. 'The CTS-R, how the Client is working and when they develop new learning'. 'The therapeutic relationship'.

P3. 'I can feel it'. 'Feedback from Clients'.

P4. 'How I feel'.

P5. 'Videoing sessions and feedback from Clients'.

P6. 'Client feedback'.

P7. 'A felt sense'. 'Client feedback, they get better, they return'.

P8. 'Feedback from Clients, they come back'.

P9. 'Client feedback'.

A clear theme here is how the trainee has accessed their interpersonal processes to measure their skills in CBT and there is only one reference made to the CTS-R. Client feedback played a significant role within these appraisals of trainee skills again highlighting the importance of the therapeutic alliance and what the trainee sought when identifying if they were competent or not. There are still references made to the Client returning to therapy which some trainees felt was an indicator to measure and reassure their competence as therapists. So both internal (a felt sense) and external (The Client giving feedback and coming back for therapy) seem to be variables here with regards to influencing trainee perception of their competence. In light of this, it seems apparent that the trainee *needs* feedback as an indicator of ability and measure of skill but these are their own interpersonal processes (assumptions) and the motivational behaviour of the Client who returns to treatment and may offer positive comments to the trainee. Of course this could be a completely false measure as some Clients may be either dependent individuals or, may not want to upset the trainee by not engaging or coming to the arranged therapy sessions. They may also falsely report improvement for the same reasons. It is unclear then that the trainees' perception and measure of competence can be taken as valid with regards to the issues highlighted. However, this need and associated cognitive processes appear to distract them from a LOTS.

The next question focuses on the skills the trainees believe are not to competent with:

Interview question:

What areas are you not so good at? – **NA, LOC and LOTS.**

P1. 'Prioritising things'. 'Reading, planning sessions, Socratic Questioning and Guided Discovery'.

P2. 'Prioritising agenda items and being assertive with Clients'.

P3. 'Agenda-setting'.

P4. 'Trauma work, reliving and leading the session'.

P5. 'Pacing, trauma processing and working with GAD'.

P6. 'PTSD, chronic anxiety and working with complex cases'.

P7. 'Goal setting, setting SMART Goals and in identifying hot cognitions'.

P8. 'Socratic Questioning, Guided Discovery and some cognitive stuff'.

P9. 'Agenda-setting, time-keeping, downward arrowing and identifying hot cognitions'.

There are two areas here which seem to cause the trainee to feel they are lacking competence (NA, LOTS). Firstly, there are several comments made regarding their ability to be able to focus and structure sessions (LOTS). Again they highlight the CTS-R as a measure of this. They also mention specific therapeutic skills such as Socratic Questioning, Guided Discovery, the processing of trauma, agenda-setting, pacing, downward arrowing and goal-setting which they feel they need to develop further (LOTS). There are also references made to difficulties working with certain disorders and again, 'complex cases' seem to be an issue for the trainee therapist (LOTS). It is somewhat reassuring in the author's opinion that the trainees' feel confident enough to discuss their perception of what areas they recognise as needing further development and consolidation. So although there are elements of anxiety/concern here (NA), it is felt that there are also hints of motivation to develop after highlighting what they perceive to be further training needs. Clearly all trainees are going to have areas in which further training and consolidation time is required, and certainly with regards to CBT practice as there are so many skills to hone. There was a felt sense of ownership here by the author as the trainees' could all identify what areas they needed to develop, but there was not a sense of blaming how they had been taught at university. So in this sense, the trainees seem to have taken responsibility for their own development as therapists beyond the scope of university teaching. One trainee mentions reading as an area in which they need to develop which further puts weight to this argument as they realise they have an obligation for self-directed study as autonomous professional practitioners. Obviously the trainees' were concerned about their skills both as therapists (LOTS), but also owing the demands of the services in which they worked (LOC).

The following question was a directed at eliciting whether the trainees found the training adequate to be able to practice as therapists:

Do you think your training helped make you competent enough to do your job? – **NA, LOTS and LOC.**

P1. 'No, I think you need a lot of background knowledge in CBT to begin with'.

P2. 'The training is not enough on its own'.

P3. 'It's like you have the arm-bands but are not yet ready for the water'.

P4. 'Not fully competent yet'. 'I need more time to consolidate learning'.

P5. 'I need to work with other disorders which I have not been able to yet'.

P6. 'Yes'.

P7. 'Yes'.

P8. 'I feel anxious about it, but I do feel I can work competently but I know I need to develop in certain areas'.

P9. 'No'. 'I need more supervision'.

What seems apparent here is the student's apprehension with regards to working as full-time therapists now the training has ended (NA). Certainly the comments made about 'not being ready for the water without arm-bands' is indicative of the trainee in this case having a fear of 'drowning' so to speak (NA, LOTS, LOC). This could be perceived as the trainee feeling overwhelmed with the work ahead and the expectations from the organisation as highlighted in earlier questions (LOC). One trainee reported to wanting access to Clients with particular disorders but had not yet been able to receive these cases (LOC). There is also a theme throughout with the trainee wanting 'more' in certain areas of teaching and support (LOTS). Realistically speaking this could not be managed by the university or clinical placement as each individual trainee as highlighted wants 'more of something' in different areas. This obviously could not be accommodated without significantly extending the training period in the author's opinion. With regards to needing more supervision, the trainees on the IAPT Programme receive weekly supervision both at university and clinical placement so one could question in light of this request if these particular trainees' are actually competent to practice as a therapist, or, whether their perception is that they are not (LOTS). It does seem apparent in light of these anxieties that some trainees will need more reassurances than others pertaining to their abilities. Other trainees however seem to feel ready to practice, but conversely, they may well be over-estimating their abilities here. It is somewhat difficult therefore to accurately identify who is ready and who is not yet ready for full-time clinical practice as therapists regardless of trainees' passing the course. i.e. their own perception of competence can differ widely from that of the assessors and markers.

There seems to be quite a 'mixed bag' of emotions apparent with all trainees'. They seem to have both elements of anxiety *and* happiness – The Happy Anxious Trainee? Most students thought they had a good level of teaching although this did not mirror what the organisation expected from them as therapists. One student commented on receiving a lot of confidence from the teaching staff, but felt there was no confidence in them at their clinical placement. One trainee felt that they were made to practice **'watered down therapy', 'It's Lidl therapy instead of Marks's'.** There was also some anger directed at 'IAPT' by one trainee who stated, **'IAPT didn't deliver what was promised'. 'If IAPT was a person I would torture them'.** This particular trainee seemed to feel anger towards a perception of being betrayed or fooled in some way. It could be argued they trusted and believed in what the IAPT Programme stated it would provide, but in some light it did not deliver the goods for them so to speak. With the discrepancies highlighted between the theory and practice areas (theory-practice gap) it could be assumed the trainee may feel duped in some way owing to this.
Another trainee was very anxious and apprehensive with regards to commencing full-time clinical work, **'I feel a sense of dread now going into full-time clinical working'. 'I feel performance will be monitored constantly'. 'We never get good feedback only bad and I feel under pressure at work'.** This trainee does seem to be very fearful of entering the work-place as a therapist and again there seems to be a lot of anticipatory anxiety surrounding this. There also seems to be some distrust pertaining to the organisation and almost a fear of being 'found out' in some way that they are not competent and could be dismissed as a result. So all three themes of Negative Affect, Loss of Therapist Self and Loss of Control seem to be apparent here and do effect the trainees' perception of competence when they are asked about their abilities to practice as therapists.

Results and Discussion

The current study highlighted similar issues found by Milne (1985) in that the participants reported how the training did not always reflect what was required of them as therapists in the IAPT Service. This was owing to them being faced with Clients with complex and comorbid disorders that they felt did not 'fit' into the treatment models they had been taught to use after one year of study. Whilst trauma-focused approaches are taught on the course, Rollinson et al (2007) and Shafran et al, (2009) argue that further training is required in this and other areas, so it is not surprising therefore that the newly qualified therapists have anxiety about their ability to practice. Indeed several participants reported to working with Clients with post-traumatic stress disorder and did not feel confident in their skills in this area. There was a lot of confusion regarding how to formulate treatment plans and this caused the participants a lot of anxiety and they began to question their abilities. There were also anxieties associated with being dismissed because they would not be able to do the job effectively or be able to perform in the time-limited way expected of them. Together with this, there were Clients they were expected to see by the organisation who did not specifically meet the criteria for depression and anxiety which is what the training was geared towards, and highlighted in the Layard Report. Another common concern was the amount of sessions they would be 'allowed' in which to help the Clients. They were allowed a maximum of 12 sessions and they felt that for the majority of Clients this was not enough therapy to make any significant progress for their presenting problems.

The problem here is highlighted by Shafran et al (2009) who state the research in CBT involves recruiting participants who do not match with the presentations of the Clients referred to clinical practice owing to strict inclusion/exclusion criteria. However, it is further highlighted several trials have taken place involving participants with comorbidities and have recruited participants who match those referred to routine clinical practice (Weisz, Weersing, and Henggeler, 2005 Wilson, 2007; DeRubeis et al, 2005). The majority of the participants in the author's study did not state this to be the case and reported the Clients they were seeing in practice were 'complex'. They thought several of the Clients should be seen by a Psychologist or referred to Step Four, in line with the Stepped Care Model (NIMHE, 2007; 2011). However, NIMHE also state that the Client should receive the least intrusive intervention for their issues (NIMHE, 2011), so this does create some confusion for both the trainee and experienced therapist working in an IAPT Service, when considering who to treat with CBT or whether to step the Client up or down. Shafran et al (2009) further argue that there needs to be measures put into place to identify which Clients would benefit from lower-intensity interventions and those who would require face-to-face therapy. Another issue however appears to be some difficulties some of the trainees' highlighted with regards to Clients being accepted for treatment once referred to Step Four Services. It seems there were elements of frustration and anxiety and a feeling that the trainee should 'hold on' to the Client as they did not know what to do with them and may have had concerns about risk and their responsibility as clinicians to 'do something' for the Client. Clearly theses are cases one would expect to be taken to supervision, but if there are organisational problems with regards to Client care pathways then this needs to be explored and addressed in the author's opinion.

A concern that arose several times during the interviews with participants was the levels of stress they were experiencing due to course-work and the demands of the organisations they worked for. Thompson et al (2011) state professional counsellors and more so with those in training, are at a high risk of burnout owing to the overwhelming needs of the Clients and heavy caseloads. Some comments were made regarding the need for personal support in this area for trainees including personal therapy which may be implemented in the training curriculum as is the case with counselling courses.

The trainees' appeared to interpret their experiences of training in CBT as 'an emotional rollercoaster'. They seemed to access different emotions in answer to the questions at interview. Questions geared towards their competence seemed to elicit feelings of anxiety, and frustration. Questions highlighting organisational issues (although non-intentional) appeared to elicit feelings of anger and fear. Questions regarding teaching and the course curricular appeared to elicit feelings of being overwhelmed, anxiety, confusion and frustration. There is clearly a Loss of Therapist Self within this process as some trainees seemed to indicate a loss of identity of who they were and had confusion regarding clinical practice caused by university teaching and organisational expectations. Although questions were not specifically asked about the trainees' organisations, there were several references made to their clinical placements which were mainly negative in nature. This Negative Affect appeared to be due the Loss of Control they reported regarding what they needed from the IAPT Services to be allowed to work effectively as therapists. It might have been worthwhile exploring these specific issues more in-depth to examine the trainees' meanings of working in this pressurised environment. The author feels the organisations certainly affected the trainees' perception of competence in light of the many negative references made towards them without prompting.

Prior to the introduction of the IAPT Programme there were obviously far fewer CB Therapists practicing in the NHS. As a Clinical Psychologist once said to the author, 'Cognitive Behavioural Therapists are like budgie teeth, you can't get them'. The older therapists seem to hold onto their roles for many years. Further research may be warranted to see if in the future there is a much larger turnover of therapists working for the NHS and if the experiences highlighted here have been a cause for this. Of course this is complete speculation but the flavour of emotion the author perceived from the trainees appeared to indicate a mostly unhappy group who did not present as individuals wanting to continue working as therapists for the NHS if at all. The author argues that this shift is mainly associated with the current NHS climate and not that of the training establishment. For example the Francis Report (Francis, 2013) found poor standards of care and low staff morale when investigating complaints at the Mid Staffordshire NHS Foundation Trust. Measures have been put in place to improve standards of care and to give staff more of a voice with regards to delivering quality services. However, with newly qualified therapists feeling a loss of control regarding their practice, it could be assumed that they do not have the voice suggested from the inquiry. One may also argue if everyone is to receive up to 12-sessions of CBT in the IAPT Services could this be viewed as 'quality of care? The author feels the university in this case delivered the IAPT Programme very well and the trainees' all seemed to have a good understanding of the theory and practice of CBT. However, they seem to have appraised this or taken their experiences to mean they are not competent or ready to work as full time therapists in the IAPT Services.

Many of the trainees' experienced a sense of loss or losses which has been presented here, but one of the major losses may have come from the realisation that teaching was coming to an end and they would now have to work as therapists without this support. This in turn may well have produced Negative Affect and a Loss of Control. The Loss of the Therapist Self would also be evident as they were now entering the organisation full time in which a lot of negatives were expressed.

With regards to personality-types and those people who choose to train as therapists, Barnett (2007) interviewed nine experienced therapists to consider their personal and professional histories. Two major themes emerged of early loss and narcissistic needs, which highlighted the concept of the 'wounded healer'. If one were to generalise this concept, it could be argued that therapists, or certainly trainee therapists may be vulnerable and more likely to react emotionally to feelings of loss.

Although this study highlighted the service-demand characteristics as a cause for the trainees' affect, one cannot rule out the possible interpersonal vulnerabilities of some trainees. Halewood and Tribe (2010) studied trainee counselling Psychologists to ascertain the level of narcissistic injury reported when working with Clients. Results indicated there were high levels of narcissistic injury reported by the trainees. It is suggested that this can interfere with Client work, can cause an increase in drop-out rates and burnout for the therapists concerned. So one could consider if some trainees' do have a vulnerability to narcissistic injury then this too could be a variable affecting how they perceive their competence and training experiences.

Similarities to this study were found in an earlier work by Nel (2006). Six Family Therapy Trainees were interviewed and data was analysed using IPA. The results suggested that the trainees' appraised their training to be overwhelming and de-skilling which in turn provoked a re-evaluation of their personal, relational and professional identities. So it does appear the trainee proceeds through a normal process of 'uncomfortable change' on both personal and interpersonal levels.

Conclusion, Recommendations and Limitations

This study has highlighted several issues and a good proportion of positive elements of the trainees' experiences of the PgDip CBT programme and their experiences of working in the 'real world' in an IAPT Service.

Some of the trainees' felt anxious and unprepared to enter full-time clinical practice and felt ill-equipped to deal with the Clients which were referred to them. They did not feel the training was long enough and would have liked to have seen more demonstrations of live therapy sessions by experts in CBT, including those sessions that did not go too well. Basically they wanted a taste of how to work with complex Clients as they felt that this was a true reflection of what they were working with in the IAPT Services. There were some expressions of anger and frustration owing to these issues and they felt the training 'promised' one thing, but never delivered the true reflection of working in the real world of Primary Care. With regards to working within the time-limited 12 session format, they felt this was an inadequate amount of therapy to be expected to make much progress with the Clients they saw on the whole. This in turn caused the trainees' to feel frustrated and unsupported by their employers.

The trainees' found supervision to be helpful and also found the Master Classes to be useful in their learning. The length of the course they would have liked to be extended to 18-months and they would have liked to have more input in certain disorders and treatment protocols.

They also felt that they commenced CBT practice too early and found it difficult and anxiety evoking that they had to see four Clients per day. They felt two Clients a day would have been more beneficial for their planning of sessions and reflective practice following them. Some of the trainees' thought engaging in personal CBT themselves would have been helpful during the course and could be included within the curriculum.

As treatment in Primary Care is now time-limited to have the best trained practitioners would be the most cost-effective and viable option in the author's opinion. With regards to Client care and clinical outcome measures, offering the Client the best possible chance of recovery could be addressed if trainees' were highly skilled and confident upon completion of their training. The new training programme is very intense and is completed over one year involving a large volume of material they had to learn, practice and consolidate to be able to work in Primary Care as therapists. Supervision was reported to be good but this still was not enough to alleviate the trainees' anxieties regarding their abilities. They did however receive a lot of supervision so it could be argued that the trainees' expectations from the course were somewhat unrealistic. Indeed, earlier or 'old school' training did not accommodate as much trainee input as with the IAPT Programme, but most of the older courses were longer in duration. In the author's training there was a module on 'the wider aspects of CBT' which did allow for stretching the scope of CBT practice to work more transdiagnostically with complex cases. In this module the author worked with a prisoner on trial for the double murders of his parents' who was diagnosed with narcissistic personality disorder which was obviously a complex case for a trainee, but with expert and close supervision was able to work effectively with this particular Client. So it may be helpful for the trainee in the IAPT Programme to be encouraged to work with the wider applications of CBT, i.e. complex cases with the added teaching and supervision in this focused area.

A lot of the issues the trainees' experienced were essentially 'normal' and this has been shown in several studies for the newly qualified practitioner in a variety of fields. It would be pertinent to evaluate courses of a longer length than the IAPT CBT course to see if there was a difference in the trainees' experiences. It would also be interesting to examine if trainees' on other IAPT CBT Courses around the country would have given the same accounts as those in this study, to understand whether the issues identified here have only local relevance

This study was conducted with a small population so it could be argued a better picture of the trainees' experiences could have been captured with larger populations and from different Universities and NHS Trusts. However, IPA can elicit enough information from small populations (Smith et al, 1999). Also, there were no follow up interviews planned with the trainees' which may have provided some useful data. For example, after some time practicing and consolidating their clinical practice it could be assumed their anxieties would subside and they would find a more relaxed way of working with the vast majority of Clients referred to them. They may well have developed their own area of expertise and owing to this, may feel less incompetent regarding their abilities to practice as therapists'. That being said, they may also reflect on the training they had received and their views regarding this may also alter when they realise that in fact what they experienced was a normal process, and the training was adequate as they find themselves still employed and functioning well in the IAPT Services. It could also be questioned if the Clients they deemed too 'complex' during their training were evaluated as less difficult to work with once they were more experienced.

Of course the data gathered here is merely an interpretation of what the author thinks is relevant and may well be biased to some degree. The author is a cognitive behavioural therapist who has been practicing for some time now in an IAPT Service and also Primary Care Mental Health Service prior to this. The training the author received was non-IAPT and took a different format including a residential training block and teaching on the wider applications of CBT. There was also a personal, experiential component to the training which took the form of 'doing CBT on the self'. The author, although not consciously aware, may be biased into thinking the earlier training was more effective. Likewise, those older and more experienced clinicians in CBT may well think that their training was more effective than that of the authors and the trainees' studying the current IAPT Programme. Although out of the scope of this paper, this may be an interesting next step for an exploratory study in the author's opinion.

The author is also a Mental Health Nurse (MHN), so may also be biased into thinking MHNs' make better therapists, although again this is not something the author is aware of. It is hoped the data here has been analysed with a 'clear and enquiring mind'. It is also hoped therefore that the above biases may have been either absent or reduced significantly to not affect the analysis.

With regards to the participants under study, one cannot rule out the possible bias of the Hawthorn or Observer Effect. Indeed, it was found following a series of experiments carried out by Professor Elton Mayo and his team, beginning in 1927 at the Hawthorne plant of the Western Electrical Company in Chicago, workers' productivity increased when under study (Gillespie, 1993). The argument put forward after these observations was that people under study, and who are receiving added attention may behave in ways out of the norm (Gillespie,

1993). An example of this in this current study may be certain trainees' exaggerating their abilities as therapists and thereby not offering a true account which would in turn contaminate the data. However, the Hawthorne effect has also been shown to be seriously flawed (Merrett, 2006).

Competence is not easy to measure, it can be subjective and influenced by both internal and external factors, and there can be many of these. It is particularly difficult to define if the subject is a trainee who is experiencing high levels of negative affect. This clearly causes them to indicate a lower level of competence if they are under stress. The IAPT Programme does seem to cause the trainees a lot of stress which seems to be heightened with the theory-practice gap. The trainees in this study were all experienced practitioners in mental health before commencing this training programme so their affect levels may not as been as high as those with less experience. However, this demonstrates that no matter how experienced the trainee is in a certain field, when faced with a high-pressured training programme, they appear to begin to question their abilities which are influenced by negative affect. Conversely, there are also trainees' who feel they are competent to very competent. These particular individuals may in fact be over-evaluating their performance as therapists so again measuring ability is somewhat difficult. The author feels the CTS-R is effective in addressing this issue, again if applied by an expert[s] in CBT, but this is also a subjective measure and can be questioned regarding reliability and validity.

The author feels the IAPT Programme is short, intense and prescriptive and does not reflect CBT work in common clinical practice in the current climate of IAPT and the Stepped Care Model. Whether this is due to the training or discrepancies and none-clarity between the 'Steps' is an issue for further debate in the author's opinion. In an ideal world the course would be longer (18 months) with added curricular including working with wider applications of CBT (complex cases), transdiagnostic, or multi-model working, and the provision of personal therapy for trainees. But this is a very idealised opinion which may not fit too well with 'Governing bodies' while waiting times for therapy are quite high. As public demand increases for psychological support the subsequent effect for getting therapist trained and up and running will obviously result in shorter and condensed training courses. This will clearly affect trainees' on an emotional level which in turn will influence their views of their competence and experiences of training programmes in CBT.

It is hoped that through this research, although limited, the training and organisational establishments may consider some of the issues raised and put into place further support for trainee therapists. They apply for training in CBT because they believe in it and they come with the best intentions to train and practice as skilled practitioners. It would be a great shame if the trainee-come qualified practitioner became despondent about practicing CBT once qualified. The author feels that some 'reality' needs to be introduced into the training, i.e. theory-practice gap (as is incorporated into nurse training) so the trainee in CBT does not feel a sense of 'shock' when faced with the real world of therapy work in IAPT Services.

The author agrees with Bennet-Levy and Beedie (2007) in that trainee therapists' do have their 'ups and downs' throughout training and probably beyond when consolidating their clinical practice. It does seem the trainee tries hard to understand what they are taught, but as the volume to learn is very large, this cannot be accomplished without some negative affect being experienced by them in the author's opinion. It is assumed they will all go on to hone their skills in the clinical environments and develop those areas of practice they consider to be lacking with appropriate supervision. They may still question their effectiveness as therapists at times throughout their careers. It is hoped that the experiences of their initial training will assist them to reflect upon their personal journeys and develop a realisation they overcame these anxieties and concerns and can do so again. Indeed, the interpersonal journeys they experience may make them better reflective practitioners and more effective therapists.

References

Barnett, M. (2007) What brings you here? A exploration of the unconscious motivations of those who choose to train and work as psychotherapists and counsellors. Psychodynamic Practice: Individuals, Groups and Organisations. 13.**3**. 257-274.

Benner, P. (1987) Clinical judgement: How expert nurses use intuition. American Journal of Nursing. 87.**1**. 23-31.

Bennet-Levy, J & Beedie, A. (2007) The Ups and Downs of Cognitive Therapy Training: What Happens to Trainees Perceptions of Their Competence During a Cognitive Therapy Training Course? Behavioural and Cognitive Psychotherapy. 35.61-75.

Bennett-Levy, J; McManus, F; Westling, B.E; & Fennell, M. (2009) Acquiring and Refining CBT Skills and Competencies: Which Training Methods are Perceived to be Most Effective? Behavioural and Cognitive Psychotherapy. **37**. 571-583.

Borders, L.D. (1990) Developmental changes during supervisees' first practicum. The Clinical Supervisor. 8.**2**. 157-167.

Brosan, L; Reynolds, S; & Moore, R.G. (2006) Factors Associated with Competence in Cognitive Therapist. Behavioural and Cognitive Psychotherapy. **23**. 179-190.

Cashwell, T.H; & Dooley, K. (2001) The impact of supervision on counsellor self-efficacy. The Clinical Supervisor. **20**. 39-47.

Connolly, M. & Brown, T. (2009) Therapists' competence – maintenance matters too. Psychiatric Bulletin **33**. 315-316.

Conrad, P. (1987) The experience of illness: recent and new directions. Research in the Sociology of Health Care, **6**. 1-31.

DeRubeis, R.J; Hollon, S.D; Amsterdam, J.D; Shelton, R.C; Young P.R; Salomon, R.M; O'Reardon, J.P; Lovett, M.L; Gladis; M.M; Brown, L.L; & Gallop, R. (2005) Cognitive Therapy Versus Medications in the Treatment of Moderate to Severe Depression. Archives of General Psychiatry **62**. 409-416.

Davidson, K. & Scott, J. (2009) Does therapists' competence matter in delivering psychological therapy? The Psychiatrist **33**: 315-316.

Doolittle, P.E. (1997) Vygotsky's Zone of Proximal Development as a Theoretical Foundation for Cooperative Learning. Journal on Excellence in College Teaching. 8.**1**. 83-103.

Field, A. & Hole, G. (2003) How to Design and Report Experiments. London, Sage.

Francis, R. (2013) Report of the Mid Staffordshire NHS Foundation Trust Public Inquiry: Executive Summary.
http://www.midstaffspublicinquiry.com/sites/default/files/report/Executive%20summary.pdf

Gillespie, R. (1993) Manufacturing Knowledge: A History of the Hawthorne Experiments. Cambridge. Cambridge University Press.

Glen, S & Waddington, K. (1998) Role Transition from Staff Nurse to Clinical Nurse Specialist: A Case Study. Journal of Clinical Nursing. 7. 283-290.

Gonsalvez & Freestone (2007) Field Supervisors' Assessments of Trainee Performance: Are they Reliable and Valid? Australian Psychologist 46. 101-112.

Grant, A; Townend, M; & Sloan, G. (2008) The Transfer of CBT Education from Classroom to Work Setting: Getting it Right or Wasting Opportunities? The Cognitive Behaviour Therapist. 1. 27-44.

Halewood, A. & Tribe, R. (2010) What is the prevalence of narcissistic injury among trainee Counselling Psychologists. Psychology and Psychotherapy: Theory, Research and Practice. 76.1. 87-102.

James, I. A; Blackburn, I. M; & Reichelt (2001) Manual of the Revised Cognitive Therapy Scale. Newcastle Cognitive Behavioural Therapies Centre. Newcastle: University of Newcastle Upon Tyne.

Kazantzis, N. (2003) Therapist Competence in Cognitive Behavioural Therapies: Review of the Contemporary Empirical Evidence. Behaviour Change 20. 1. 1-12

Keen, J.A. & Freeston, M.H. (2008) Assessing Competence in Cognitive Behavioural Therapy. The British Journal of Psychiatry 193. 60-64.

Larkin, M., Watts, S., Clifton, E. (2006). Giving voice and making sense in Interpretative Phenomenological Analysis. Qualitative Research in Psychology, 3:2. 102-120.

Layard, R. (2006) The Depression Report: A New Deal for Depression and Anxiety. London: The Centre for Economic Performance's Mental Health Policy.

McCutcheon, H.H.I. & Pincombe, J. (2001) Intuition: an important tool in the practice of nursing. Journal of Advanced Nursing. 35.3. 342-348.

Merrett, F. (2006) Reflection on the Hawthorne Effect. Educational Psychology 26.1. 143-146.

Milne, D. (1985) A Review of the In-Service Training of Nurses in Behaviour Therapy. Behavioural Psychotherapy 13.2. 120-131.

Nel, P.W. (2006) Trainee perspectives on their Family Therapy Training. Journal of Family Therapy. 28.3. 307-328.

NIMHE (2007) New Ways of Working for Psychological Therapists: Overarching Report. London: National Institute for Mental Health in England.

NIMHE (2011) Common Mental Health Disorders: Identification and Pathways to Care. London: National Institute for Mental Health in England.

Robinson, S; Kellett, S; King, I; & Keating, V. (2012) Role Transition from Mental Health Nurse to IAPT High Intensity Psychological Therapist. Behavioural and Cognitive Psychotherapy. 40.3. 351-66

Rollinson,R; Haig, C; Warner, R; Garety P; Kuipers, E; Freeman D; Bebbington, P; Dunn, G; & Fowler, D. (2007) The application of cognitive behavioural therapy for psychosis in clinical and research settings. Psychiatry Services 58. 1297-1302.

Roth, A.D. & Pilling, S. (2008) Using an Evidence-Eased Methodology to Identify the Competencies Required to Deliver Effective Cognitive and Behavioural Therapy for Depression and Anxiety disorders. Behavioural and Cognitive Psychotherapy. 36. 129-147.

Shafran, R; Clark, D.M; Fairburn, C.G; Arntz,A; Barlow, D.H; Ehlers, A; Freeston, M; Garety, P.A; Hollon, S.D; Ost, L.G; Salkovskis, P.M; Williams, J.M.G; & Wilson, G.T. (2009) Mind the Gap: Improving the Dissemination of CBT. Behaviour Research and Therapy 47. 902-909.

Smith, J.A; Jarman, M; & Osborn, M. (1999) Doing Interpretative Phenomological Analysis. In: Murray, M. & Chamberlain, K. (Eds.) Qualitative Health Psychology London: Sage.

Smith, J.A. & Osborn, M. (2003) Interpretative Phenomological Analysis. In: Smith, J.A. (Ed) Qualitative Psychology: A Practical Guide to Methods. London. Sage.

Smith, J.A; Flowers, P; & Larkin, M. (2009) Interpretative Phenomological Analysis: Theory, Method and Research. London. Sage.

Thompson, E.H; Frick, M.H; & Trice-Black, S. (2011) Counsellor in training perceptions of supervision practices related to self-care and burnout. The Professional Counsellor. 1.3. 152-162.

Trepka, C; Rees, A; Shapiro, D.A; Hardy, G.E; & Barkham, M. (2004) Therapist Competence and Outcome of Cognitive Therapy for depression. Cognitive Therapy and Research. 28. 2. 143-157.

Truman, P. (2003) Intuition and practice. Nursing Standard. 18.7. 42-43.

Weisz, J.R; Weersing, V.R; & Henggleler, S.W. (2005) Jousting with Straw Men: Comment on the Westen, Novotny, and Thompson-Brenner (2004) Critique of Empirically Supported Treatments. Psychological Bulletin 131. 418-426, discussion 427-433.

Zivor, M; Salkovskis, P.M; Oldfiled, V.B; & Kushnir, J. (2013) Formulation in Cognitive Behavior Therapy for Obsessive–Compulsive Disorder: Aligning Therapists, Perceptions and Practice. Clinical Psychology: Science and Practice 20.2. 143-151.